What Do We Know About Zombies?

by Meg Belviso

illustrated by Andrew Thomson

Penguin Workshop

For Dylan Quinn Campanella—MB

For Rhia, Cerys, and Esme—AT

PENGUIN WORKSHOP
An imprint of Penguin Random House LLC
1745 Broadway, New York, New York 10019

First published in the United States of America by Penguin Workshop,
an imprint of Penguin Random House LLC, 2025

Visit us online at penguinrandomhouse.com.

Library of Congress Cataloging-in-Publication Data is available.

Printed in the United States of America

ISBN 9780593889893 (paperback)   10 9 8 7 6 5 4 3 2   CJKW
ISBN 9780593889909 (library binding)   10 9 8 7 6 5 4 3 2 1 CJKW

Contents

What Do We Know About Zombies?

On October 1, 1968, an audience of all ages settled into their seats in the Fulton Theater in Pittsburgh, Pennsylvania, for the premiere of a new film called *Night of the Living Dead*. At that time, movies did not yet have the ratings system we have today, which lets audiences know which movies are okay for kids to see.

Many of the people in the theater were teenagers and younger children. They had enjoyed plenty of fun scary movies, and were eager to see a new one. The lights went down and the movie began.

On screen, a girl named Barbra and her brother, Johnny, visited their father's grave in rural Pennsylvania, not too far from the very theater where the movie was playing. Barbra's brother made fun of her for being afraid of the spooky graveyard. As they laid some flowers on the ground, lightning flashed. They saw a man lurching and stumbling among the gravestones. "They're coming to get you, Barbra!" Johnny teased her as the man came closer.

But it turns out that the man in the graveyard really *was* coming to get her. He was a dead person who had come back to life. He wanted to attack and eat them both. Barbra and Johnny had never heard of such a creature before and until that day in 1968, the movie audience had never heard of the concept of the living dead, either. While stories about vampires and werewolves had been around for hundreds of years, this shuffling, groaning, hungry monster had never been seen before.

Night of the Living Dead was much too scary for many of the younger kids in the theater. They weren't even sure what these monsters were called.

In the months that followed, fans of the movie would start calling them *zombies*. That name came

from a totally different kind of walking dead. The
original zombie didn't bite, it didn't growl, and it
didn't eat people. The idea for this creature came
from a Caribbean country called Haiti.

CHAPTER 1
The Magic Island

People disagree on the exact origin of the word *zombie*. But it became widely known in the United States thanks to a man named William Seabrook, who published a book called *The Magic Island* in 1929. The book was about his travels in

William Seabrook

Haiti, a nation that shares the island of Hispaniola with the Dominican Republic in the Caribbean Sea, east of Cuba and Jamaica.

At the time Seabrook visited Haiti, it was an independent country. Before that, it had been a colony, first of Spain, and then of France. A colony is a country controlled by a more powerful one, which often uses the colony's natural resources to enrich itself.

Many valuable products, including sugar, coffee, indigo, cacao, and cotton, were once grown and harvested by enslaved people in Haiti. Slavery officially ended in Haiti in 1805. But before it did, most of the people in Haiti—sometimes as much as 90 percent of the population—were enslaved.

Fieldwork and other labor in Haiti was so difficult that the enslaved workers longed to be free of it, even if they had to die to do so. However, some whispered that even death might not free them. They told stories of people who rose out of their graves as zombies—empty human shells without souls who returned to the fields like puppets who didn't control their own bodies. A zombie had to do anything its master wanted them to do. Some say the enslavers themselves spread these stories to scare people out of trying to become free. They knew the worst thing their workers could imagine was being enslaved even after death.

Hispaniola

The island that Haiti sits on is four hundred miles long and one hundred and fifty miles wide. When Christopher Columbus landed there in 1492, he claimed the whole island for Spain and named it *Hispaniola*, which meant *Spanish Island*. Over the next few centuries, French settlers came to Hispaniola, too.

By 1697, the northwestern part of the island was controlled by France, who called it *Saint-Domingue*. It eventually became the country of Haiti. The rest of the island is now the territory of the Dominican Republic. The official language of the Dominican Republic is Spanish. The official languages of Haiti are French and Haitian Creole. Each country speaks the language of the larger one that originally colonized it.

William Seabrook was a journalist who traveled to places most Americans had never seen. He wrote stories that made them seem very exciting and mysterious. His descriptions of Haiti were no different.

One chapter of *The Magic Island* in particular got a lot of attention. It was called ". . . Dead Men Working in the Cane Fields."

In it, Seabrook said he'd visited a field owned by an American sugar company that hired local people to work for it. Some of these workers looked strange to Seabrook. They shuffled when they walked. They didn't speak. Their eyes seemed dull and lifeless. All these things could be explained by the exhausting work they were doing in the hot sun.

But Seabrook claimed he was told they were "zombies." A zombie was said to be the body of a person who had died and then been brought back to life to work for the sugar company.

Even though slavery had ended more than one hundred years before Seabrook wrote his book, people in Haiti still told stories about zombies forced to work or even commit crimes for the person who controlled them. People in Haiti didn't really fear being hurt by zombies. They were afraid of becoming one themselves. They hoped that if they were ever turned into a zombie, someone would feed them salt. It was said that the taste of salt would make a zombie return to their grave.

When *The Magic Island* was published in the United States,

it became a bestseller. American readers were fascinated by these creatures called zombies and the strange power that was needed to create and control them.

CHAPTER 2
Vodou

Haiti was a colony of France from 1659 to 1804. During that time, the French passed a law saying that every enslaved worker had to be baptized into France's official religion, Catholicism. Once a person was baptized as Catholic, they were taught about their new faith and ordered to give up any religious beliefs they had before.

As life for enslaved people in Haiti was so difficult, their lives were often very short. New people were constantly being enslaved and brought to Haiti to fill the need for labor. Usually, those people were taken from the African continent. They brought with them their beliefs and rituals.

The enslaved workers didn't all come from the exact same part of Africa, and didn't all share

the exact same ideas. But their beliefs had more in common with each other than with the Catholic faith of France. Over time, the enslaved people created their own religion by combining different traditions into something new. This new religion was

An illustration by Alexander King from *The Magic Island*

called Vodou. It was practiced in secret because it was against the law for anyone in the colony to be anything other than Catholic.

There is only one god in Vodou, called Bondye, which means "good god." There are also thousands of spirits, called *loa* (or *lwa*). The loa have mysterious powers. They can heal illness and protect people from harm, punish those who do wrong, and give people advice to guide them to good fortune. They can even guide a revolution to victory. The loa sometimes speak through dreams or provide signs for religious leaders to interpret. Vodou priests are called *oungans*. Priestesses are called *manbos*. They often lead ceremonies with drumming and dancing. During these ceremonies, people can be taken over by the loa spirits to speak for them or do their will.

Haitian Revolution (1791–1804)

On the night of August 21, 1791, thousands of Haiti's enslaved workers snuck away to a secret Vodou ceremony. At that time, the country was still a French colony called Saint-Domingue. The leaders of the meeting were planning something shocking. They wanted to rise up against their French colonizers and claim their home for themselves. It was a stormy night full of thunder and lightning. The violent weather must have seemed like the loas' way of telling them they would succeed. Inspired by the ideas they heard at the meeting, the participants began attacking their enslavers and burning their houses. News of the revolt quickly spread. Within weeks a hundred thousand enslaved people had joined the fight against the French.

The war was fought off and on for thirteen years

and ended with Haiti becoming a free country. The Haitian Revolution remains the only successful slave revolt in history.

The loa spirits were a source of great magical power, and great power could be dangerous. Some Vodou leaders refused to do anything

The death loa spirit

for the loa that they considered destructive or wrong. Others chose to serve the loa "with both hands." That meant they were willing to do magic that could be dangerous or scary. Those priests are called *bokors*, and the priestesses *caplatas*.

A houngan or a manbo would not make a zombie. That is the kind of magic that only a bokor or a caplata would do.

By the time William Seabrook published *The Magic Island* in 1929, some people in the United

States—but very few—were already familiar with Vodou. During the Haitian Revolution, many French slaveowners had fled their country, bringing enslaved people with them. Those slaves introduced their religion to people in the United States, especially in New Orleans, Louisiana.

The practice of Vodou became so widespread in the city of New Orleans that it developed into its own special version with its own spelling: voodoo. A visitor to New Orleans today can see the Voodoo Spiritual Temple there, as well as a historic museum of voodoo.

Voodoo Spiritual Temple

Marie Laveau (1801–1881)

Marie Catherine Laveau was one of the most famous American followers of voodoo. She was born in New Orleans to a single mother. Although slavery was still legal in the United States at that time, Marie's mother was a free black woman. Marie became the leader of New Orleans's voodoo community, and was often called the "Voodoo Queen." It was said she could predict the future. She worked as a healer and sold charms to protect people from danger. Today, tourists and believers visit her tomb in St. Louis Cemetery No. 1 in New Orleans to make wishes on it, believing she still has the power to grant them.

Vodou is still practiced all over the world by millions of people. It is intended to bring healing and comfort, beauty and joy to the world. To many outside the faith, however, Vodou remains the same scary and mysterious tradition that William Seabrook wrote about in his book.

Seabrook's book inspired other authors to write their own stories about zombies created by magic. There was even a play called *Zombie*

BILTMORE THEATRE
ZOMBIE

The playbill for *Zombie*

on Broadway for a short time in 1932. Once Seabrook's zombies had shuffled from the page to the stage, it wasn't surprising that they would go on to conquer the silver screen.

CHAPTER 3
Going Hollywood

Two of the most popular films in the early 1930s were about monsters. Audiences loved *Frankenstein* and *Dracula*, which were both released by Universal in 1931. Hollywood studios were eager to find another on-screen monster success. Why not zombies?

Frankenstein's . . . Zombie?

Frankenstein; or, The Modern Prometheus, a book by Mary Shelley, was first published in 1818. It tells the story of a scientist who raids graveyards to steal body parts. He sews them together and brings them to life using his own scientific theories. Some people wonder if that means Frankenstein's monster is a zombie. He is not.

This monster was never a single person who died. He was constructed from different people's body parts to make a new creature. Once Victor Frankenstein brings him to life, the creature can be killed like any living person. While audiences often call the monster Frankenstein, that name actually only belongs to the scientist who made him.

White Zombie was released by United Artists in 1932. It was shot in less than eleven days for $100,000, which would be more than $2 million today. In the movie, a young woman named Madeline travels to Haiti to get married. Her fiancé is an American man who does business with a

sugar plantation there. When the plantation owner falls in love with Madeline, he asks a man named Murder Legendre to turn Madeline into a zombie that he can control, so she will love him. Legendre himself runs a sugar mill operated entirely by zombies, and he's turned most of his business rivals into zombies, too.

Although the Haitian characters in the movie all know what zombies are, the movie never calls

Legendre a bokor, and it never mentions Vodou. It presents Legendre as an evil man with mysterious powers strong enough to create zombies and Haiti as a strange place where such things could happen.

Madeline is given a potion at her wedding that appears to kill her. But after she's buried, her fiancé thinks he glimpses her walking around as if in a trance. He visits her tomb, finds it empty, and vows to save her from Legendre.

The creatures in *White Zombie* already looked a little like the zombies we see in movies today. They stared straight ahead, as if not seeing anything, and shuffled slowly when they walked. At the movie's premiere, the studio hired actors to shuffle on top of the roof of the theater, right over the lighted sign showing the name of the movie.

But the movie's zombie heroine, Madeline,

wasn't a monster. She, along with the workers at the sugar mill, were victims of the villain Legendre, who used his powers to control others. The movie didn't explain exactly how he created zombies, but he was in fact the real danger.

The character Murder Legendre in *White Zombie*

Although many people went to see *White Zombie*, it wasn't as popular as Universal's *Dracula* and *Frankenstein*. Hollywood didn't make

another big zombie movie again until 1943, when an executive at RKO movie studios saw an article in a magazine about Vodou titled "I Walked with a Zombie" and told one of his producers  to make a movie with that title.

It was shot in less than a month with a budget of only $150,000. In the movie, a young nurse named Betsy takes a job caring for the wife of a plantation owner. The plantation is on a fictional island called Saint Sebastian that seemed to be based on the culture of Haiti. Once there, Betsy discovers that her patient isn't sick at all. She's actually been turned into a zombie. Betsy visits a Vodou temple to try to find a cure for her.

Saint Sebastian, like Haiti, had a history of slavery that was linked to the fear of becoming a zombie. A character in the movie tells Betsy that the residents of the island still cry at the births of children and laugh at funerals, because under slavery, death meant freedom.

The movie includes dance scenes in Vodou ceremonies, and an actual Haitian Vodou song. But it didn't do much to change American moviegoers' impressions of Vodou. Many people still didn't respect Vodou as a religion. They thought of it as a form of black magic—sorcery that called on spirits for supernatural or evil purposes.

Dance scene from *I Walked with a Zombie*

Like *White Zombie*, *I Walked with a Zombie* failed to become as popular as *Dracula* or *Frankenstein*. Hollywood again lost interest in the zombie. But some of the elements we see in modern zombie stories were already beginning to appear in other movies. They would lay the groundwork for the hordes of walking dead we know today.

CHAPTER 4
Pod People

In the 1956 movie *Invasion of the Body Snatchers*, small-town doctor Miles Bennell has a lot of patients with the same strange problem. They believe that people they know— family and friends they see every day—have been replaced by strangers who look and sound exactly like them. Miles thinks they're imagining things, until a friend calls him to look at something he found in his house. It appears to be a dead person, but has no face or fingerprints. Before their eyes, the faceless body starts to change. It becomes an exact copy of Miles's friend.

Miles later finds an exact copy of himself growing in his greenhouse! He can see that the body has hatched out of a giant seedpod.

On the movie set of *Invasion of the Body Snatchers*, 1956

He realizes that strange plants that may have come from outer space are growing into copies of everyone in his small town and replacing them in their sleep.

These replacements, or "pod people" as they came to be called, looked human, but didn't show or feel any emotion. They were a lot like zombies who'd come back to life without their souls and personalities. One by one, everyone Miles knows joins the ranks of the pod people, until he's completely surrounded by enemies who look like his friends.

Greenhouse scene from 1956's *Invasion of the Body Snatchers*

The monsters of *Invasion of the Body Snatchers* weren't zombies. They weren't dead people brought back to life. However, the movie did show many of the elements we know from zombie movies. Not only are Miles's own friends now enemies, but Miles is terrified of turning into a pod person himself if he falls asleep. What's more, these alien pod people seem to be planning to take over the whole world.

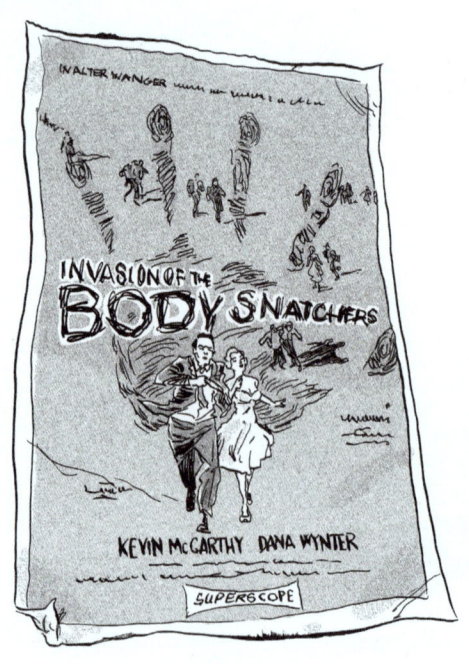

Invasion of the Body Snatchers wasn't expected to be a big hit. It was based on the 1954 book *The Body Snatchers*, written by Jack Finney. But the movie really struck a chord with audiences. It earned $1 million— that would be more than $11 million today—in just one month! It went

on to be considered one of the best science fiction movies ever, and it's been remade several times. The fear of being the only human being left when everyone around you is turning into a monster was drawing audiences.

Another film took this idea one step further. In 1964's *The Last Man on Earth*, Dr. Robert Morgan is the only human left alive after everyone else has turned into vampires. Even his own wife rose from her grave to try to kill him.

Now he is completely alone. By day, he hunts down sleeping vampires and kills them. By night, he locks himself inside his house.

The movie was based on the 1954 book *I Am Legend*, by Richard Matheson. But where the hero of *Body Snatchers* desperately tried to stop an invasion of the earth, the hero of *The Last Man on Earth* lives in a world that's already been taken over by the undead. The story takes place after an apocalypse (say: a-POCK-a-lips)—an event where the world as we know it has been destroyed. In this story, nearly everyone has been turned into a vampire.

Scene from *The Last Man on Earth*, 1964

Many of the things we take for granted, like grocery stores, telephones, and hospitals, have disappeared from Robert Morgan's world, and he has to find primitive ways to survive. Robert is incredibly lonely, and has become more violent than he ever was when he lived among living human beings. In some ways, he's become a monster himself.

Like *Body Snatchers*, *The Last Man on Earth* had a small budget. It was shot in Italy to save money and was not a big hit when it came out, but today it's considered a minor classic. Like *Body Snatchers*, it's been remade several times. The story of a single man protecting himself against an undead world continues to fascinate people and influence zombie movies to this day.

These two films created a template for many of the zombie movies that would follow. There were still some important things missing, though.

Vincent Price, as Robert, struggles with zombies
in *The Last Man on Earth*, 1964

The pod people of *Body Snatchers* and the
vampires of *Last Man* did not look dead. There
were no decaying corpses on-screen in the 1950s
and '60s. But they could be found somewhere
else—in comic books. Horror comics in the
1950s contained spine-chilling and often bloody
illustrations.

In one horror comic story, "Till Death," a man living in Haiti is so sad when his wife dies that local people bring her back to life as a zombie. The man is thrilled—until his wife's  body starts to decay, and he finds himself getting a good-morning kiss from a smelly rotting corpse buzzing with flies!

EC's horror comics were very popular with kids in the 1950s. One EC fan, a boy living in the Bronx, New York City, would grow up to create a brand-new look for monsters, and change the meaning of the word *zombie* forever.

EC Comics

EC, or Educational Comics, was a comics publisher founded by Maxwell Gaines in 1944. It was run by his son Bill Gaines beginning in 1947, after his father died. Bill changed the name of the company to Entertaining Comics, and began to produce suspense, science fiction, and war stories. But the most popular new titles were its horror comics: *Tales from the Crypt*, *The Vault of Horror*, and *The Haunt of Fear*. These comic books were gruesome and gory, but also full of puns and jokes.

In 1954, a psychiatrist named Fredric Wertham testified before the US Congress, blaming these types of comic books for encouraging and inspiring children's bad behavior. EC dropped all its horror magazines in 1956, but people still had fond memories of them. In 1989, the TV show *Tales from the Crypt*, based on the comics, brought the stories to a whole new audience. And in the summer of 2024, the brand was relaunched by Oni Press.

CHAPTER 5
They're Coming to Get You

In 1967, a group of filmmakers started shooting a movie in rural Pennsylvania just north of Pittsburgh. Their movie didn't have an official title yet. They called it *Monster Flick* first, before deciding on the title *Night of the Living Dead.*

The director was twenty-seven-year-old George Romero, who had written the script with his friend John Russo.

George had seen the movie *Invasion of the Body Snatchers*. The book *I Am Legend* had been a big inspiration for him. He wanted to write about how an apocalypse might start. As Matheson's story had vampires taking over the world, George wanted to do something different. He asked himself, "What if the dead stopped staying dead?"

George thought of his monsters as ghouls. To him, a zombie meant a person brought back to life by magic—not necessarily in a voodoo ceremony. In his movie, no one understood why the dead came back to life. But once the dead did, they hungered for living flesh.

George Romero (1940–2017)

George A. Romero was born and grew up in the Bronx, New York. His mother was Lithuanian and his father was born in Spain and grew up in Cuba. In 1960, George graduated from Carnegie Institute of Technology (now Carnegie Mellon University) in Pittsburgh, Pennsylvania, where he had studied art, design, and drama. He started making commercials and short films, including some for the popular children's show *Mister Rogers' Neighborhood*. Some of his movies include *Martin*, about a young man who thinks he's a vampire, and *Creepshow*, a movie based on the EC horror comics he'd grown up reading.

Why were George's ghouls so hungry? They didn't have to eat at all. They didn't need food for energy like living people. They just seemed to come out of their graves with a drive to eat. And no matter how much they ate, they were never satisfied.

A lot of the elements we know from modern zombie stories were already in the script of *Night of the Living Dead*. The plot centers on a small group of people hiding in an isolated farmhouse while hungry corpses are on the move in the outside world. Every person bitten by a zombie eventually becomes one. Even with the danger growing outside, the people under threat can't seem to stop arguing with one another about what to do.

Because the movie was made with such a small budget, *Night of the Living Dead*'s crew had to work other jobs during the day. They returned to the set at night and on weekends. They filmed for thirty days, but it took about nine months to shoot. They often had to stop to raise funds to continue. They saved money any way they could.

George used black-and-white film because at that time it was less expensive. The filmmakers were able to rent the farmhouse the characters were trapped in cheaply because it was soon going to be torn down. The blood in the movie was chocolate syrup. A local butcher donated meat and animal intestines as props for the zombies to "eat." The actors wore their own clothes, knowing they would probably be ruined by the end of the shoot. Since the script was unfinished, they often made up their own lines, too.

The Pennsylvania farmhouse used as the location
for *Night of the Living Dead*, 1968

Instead of hurting the movie, the black-and-white film and inexpensive effects made it scarier. Under George's creative direction, the film seemed more like a news report than a slick Hollywood production. It felt real, and it went on to become one of the most popular horror movies of all time.

The monsters in the movie are never given a name. But audiences quickly agreed these new monsters were zombies. And they were about to take over the world.

CHAPTER 6
A Trip to the Mall

In 1974, a friend of George Romero's invited him to a shopping mall in Pennsylvania. The company his friend worked for managed the whole complex. The mall contained lots of different stores under one roof. During the tour, George's friend joked that there were so many things for sale in the mall, a person could survive there for a long time with no help.

That made George think back on the characters of *Night of the Living Dead*, trapped in their little farmhouse for a night. What if they had an entire mall to hide in? What if they had to stay there for a long time? He imagined the whole world overrun by zombies, with a small group of surviving people totally outnumbered.

Even though *Night of the Living Dead* had been successful, George had a hard time finding a studio to give him enough money to make a sequel. He finally got help from an Italian director, Dario Argento, who was a big fan of the first movie and was excited to see more. George's friend got permission for him to film the movie in the shopping mall they'd once visited together, as long as George only filmed at night, after the mall was closed. He started shooting in November 1977,

not long before the Christmas season. Every night, before they started filming, the crew had to take down all the mall Christmas decorations, then put them back up again before morning.

This was so time-consuming that George stopped filming three weeks before Christmas and resumed after the holidays.

This new movie, *Dawn of the Dead*, took place

ten years after the events of the first one. All the things that people relied on, like hospitals and police and fire departments, no longer existed. In the film, a small group of people in Philadelphia steal a helicopter to escape the city and hide out in an empty shopping mall surrounded by zombies.

The zombies trying to get into the mall weren't attracted to the survivors inside. They were following an instinct to shop that was present when they were alive. Just as they craved food even though they didn't need to eat, they wanted to shop even though they no longer knew what to do with the things they could loot from the mall. Zombies were consumers. And they always wanted more. In this way, George thought, the zombies outside the mall were just like the living people hiding inside it. The longer they stayed in the mall, the more danger they were in. But even as more and more zombies gathered outside trying to get in, the living people didn't want to leave the stores.

The zombies in *Dawn of the Dead* looked even scarier and grosser than the ones in

the earlier movie. That was thanks to George now using color film and to his new special effects makeup artist, Tom Savini.

On its first weekend in theaters, *Dawn of the Dead* earned $900,000, and it went on to earn millions more. Other filmmakers started getting interested in flesh-eating zombies. Some even added their own ideas to zombie mythology.

In 1985, director and screenwriter Dan O'Bannon made a funny horror movie called *The Return of the Living Dead*, about zombies created by a poisonous gas invented by the US Army as a weapon. These zombies could talk and had a lot to say about George Romero's movies. They said George had gotten some things wrong. For instance, while George's zombies ate people entirely, these zombies only ate brains. They said they could feel their bodies falling apart, and eating living brains made them feel better.

So, if you ever hear someone imitating a zombie by moaning, "Braaaaains!" they are quoting *The Return of the Living Dead*, even if they don't know it.

Movies in the 1980s proved that zombies could be funny as well as scary. But then a single music video did something even more surprising. It gave zombies a chance to be the one thing it seemed they could never be: cool.

Tom Savini (1946–)

Growing up in Pittsburgh, Pennsylvania, Tom Savini's hero was the actor Lon Chaney Sr., who was known as "the man of a thousand faces" for his ability to change his appearance using makeup. He became famous for his roles as the Hunchback of Notre Dame and the Phantom of the Opera.

Tom loved experimenting with makeup on himself and his friends. He worked as a combat photographer during the Vietnam War. To distract himself from the terrible injuries he photographed, Tom thought about how he would re-create them as special effects with makeup. After returning to Pittsburgh, he started working with George Romero. The zombies he created for *Dawn of the Dead* amazed audiences. Tom went on to become one of the most famous special effects makeup artists of all time. In 2000, he founded Tom Savini's Special Make-Up Effects Program in Monessen, Pennsylvania, to teach the craft to new artists.

CHAPTER 7
Something Evil's Lurking in the Dark

For teenagers in 1983, the most important network on television was MTV, or Music Television. It showed music videos twenty-four hours a day. Artists with new songs made videos that could be shown on MTV to promote their music.

Most music videos were about three minutes long. But on Friday, December 2, MTV showed a special new video for the first time. It was thirteen minutes long—more like a very short movie than a standard video.

The song was "Thriller" by Michael Jackson, from his album of the same name. The album *Thriller* had been released a year earlier. It was the most popular album in the country for months and produced several hit songs and videos.

By November 1983, though, the album was no longer number one. Two videos had been released in March, and no one expected any new videos to be made from its songs.

But Michael Jackson had loved the movie *An American Werewolf in London*. He was so impressed by its special effects that he wanted to make a video with *American Werewolf*'s director, John Landis, and its makeup artist, Rick Baker.

Special effects in *An American Werewolf in London*

Michael knew just what music he wanted to use for the video, too. The title song, "Thriller," was about scary movies. It even featured a speech by Vincent Price, an actor with a distinctive voice who had appeared in many classic horror movies. The song seemed like the perfect match for the video Michael wanted to make.

However, Michael's record company didn't want to make a video of "Thriller." Especially not an extra-long and extra-expensive one. Most videos at the time cost about $50,000 to make. The video Michael was planning would have a budget of $1.2 million. So Michael and John Landis made a deal with MTV. If the channel helped pay for the video, Michael would film a behind-the-scenes show about it for the network to air and sell.

Behind the scenes of the "Thriller" video

Michael Jackson and John Landis

The "Thriller" video opened with Michael and an actress named Ola Ray, dressed like teenagers on a date in the 1950s. Michael asks his date to "go steady" and be his girlfriend. But when the full moon rises, he turns into a werecat (similar to a werewolf, but more like a cat than a wolf), using the kinds of special effects he'd liked so much in John Landis's movie.

The video then showed Michael and the same

girl in 1983, watching the werecat movie in a theater. Michael's date is scared and wants to leave. He sings as he walks her home. When they walk by a cemetery, the dead begin to crawl out of their graves. Too late, the girl realizes she's surrounded by zombies—including Michael himself, who has now been turned into one.

The zombies growl and shuffle toward the girl. Then they do something zombies had never ever done before. They dance!

The zombie group dance in "Thriller" was created (or choreographed) by Michael Peters,

who also played one of the zombies in the video. Peters created steps that fit the way zombies moved—shuffling and stiff. As MTV showed the video over and over throughout the day, people took the time to study the moves and learn the entire dance. It became one of the most famous videos—and dances—in the world. It's considered by many to be the best music video ever made. It's been viewed more than a billion times on YouTube.

Michael Peters

The album *Thriller* once again became number one in the country. In fact, it became the bestselling album of all time, selling more than sixty-six million copies worldwide. And it had an exciting dance troupe of zombies to thank for it!

Each year on Halloween, people dress up as zombies and perform the "Thriller" dance. Even President Barack Obama and First Lady Michelle Obama danced to the song with schoolchildren at a White House Halloween event in 2016.

Anyone can be a "Thriller" zombie for Halloween or just for fun. But could real zombies actually exist?

The "Thriller" Jacket

The costumes for "Thriller" were designed by Deborah Landis, the wife of the video's director and a well-known designer. Deborah dressed Michael in red so he would stand out against the dark nighttime background and appear taller. She created a jacket with raised shoulders, a high collar, and a black "V" on the front and back. Copies of the jacket became popular all over the world. In 2011, a man named Milton Verret bought the original jacket for $1.8 million. He called it "the greatest piece of rock and roll memorabilia in history." In May 2022, the jacket was temporarily loaned to the Rock and Roll Hall of Fame in Cleveland, Ohio.

CHAPTER 8
In the Wild

In the original stories from Haiti, a zombie would carry out the wishes of the bokor not because they were forced to do it or punished if they didn't, but because the person's own desires had been replaced by the wishes of their master. As surprising as it might seem, there are creatures in the animal kingdom who are able to do exactly that. It's how they survive.

These animals are called parasites. A parasite is a creature that lives in or on another animal, taking everything it needs to live from the other being. Not all parasites are dangerous to the animal that hosts them, but some harm or even kill their hosts.

For instance, so-called "voodoo wasps" lay

A voodoo wasp attacks
a caterpillar

their eggs under the skin of a caterpillar. The eggs feed off the caterpillar's own body. When the eggs hatch, they release larvae, babies that look like tiny worms.

Most of the larvae chew their way out of the caterpillar's skin—without killing the caterpillar. But a few larvae stay inside the caterpillar's brain, where they can actually control its behavior. The caterpillar no longer prepares to become a butterfly. Instead, it spins a cocoon around the larvae so they can grow into wasps. It even stays by the cocoon to guard it from predators. The

A caterpillar
with wasp larvae

caterpillar's primary instinct now is to protect the wasps.

Another example of a zombielike parasite is the horsehair worm, also called the hairworm. It lays its tiny eggs in water. When another insect like a grasshopper takes a drink, it swallows the eggs.

Grasshoppers may drink water, but they don't swim in it. Unless they have been infected by a hairworm.

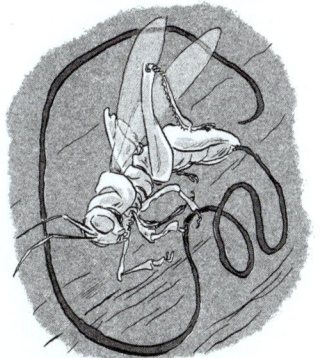

The grasshopper doesn't know there is another insect living inside it. But when it's time for

A hairworm exiting a grasshopper in water

the hairworm to lay its own eggs, the grasshopper finds the nearest body of water and jumps in. The hairworm wriggles out of the grasshopper and swims off to lay its eggs. The grasshopper has no idea why it suddenly decided to go for a swim.

It's not only insects that can be affected this

way. There is another parasite, called *Toxoplasma gondii*, that infects all sorts of animals and birds, but it only mates in one place: inside a cat. When a cat eats a bird or some other small mammal with the parasite inside it, the toxoplasma has reached its mating destination.

This parasite has a strong power over certain animals that cats like to hunt: rodents such as mice and rats. An infected mouse loses its natural fear of cats and other predators. In fact, the mouse will even start to like the smell of cats, making it easy for the cat to catch it. Once inside the cat, the toxoplasma's mating begins.

These tiny parasites, without any magic,

are able to control the behavior of much larger animals, making them do things they wouldn't choose to do themselves. But could a person ever be turned into a zombie?

People have certainly tried. In 1950, a journalist coined the word *brainwashing* to describe a process where a person's own beliefs and desires are replaced by someone else's. There's no proof that it's really possible over long periods of time, however. People, unlike grasshoppers or mice, have the ability to think about why they do things. Humans are not so easy to control.

So there's not much danger of a person being controlled as easily as a grasshopper might be. But what about the mindless shuffling monsters who infect people by biting them? Could a human be turned into something like that? As scary as it is to imagine, those types of zombies aren't completely made up.

CHAPTER 9
The World's Scariest Sickness

No dead person has ever come back to life and attacked anyone. That part of the zombie stories is made up. But there is a real disease that can turn a friendly person— or a friendly animal— into something dangerous. It's contagious and it's often spread through bites.

This disease is called rabies. For centuries, it has terrified people. Some consider it scarier than any other sickness. The first known written record of rabies is more than four thousand years old, but people must have known about the illness long before then.

Rabies is a virus. Most viruses travel through the blood. But when a person or an animal is bitten by something infected with rabies, the virus travels through the nervous system into the brain of the victim. It can take months for it to get there, but once it does, rabies can cause hallucinations and wild behavior. The victim develops a condition called hydrophobia, or "fear of water," and so they become unable to drink anything. Their mouth produces a lot of saliva or spit and the victim starts behaving strangely.

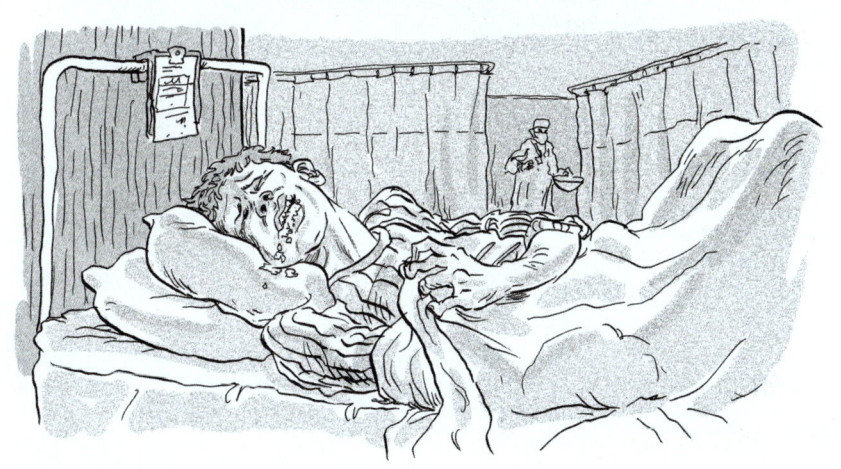

For most of history, a person or animal infected with the disease had almost no hope of surviving. Luckily, we no longer need to fear rabies the way we once did. In 1885, a vaccine for rabies was discovered. As long as a person received the series of vaccine shots before they started to show symptoms, they would be fine.

In many places, there are laws requiring pet cats and dogs to be vaccinated against rabies regularly. Today, only two or three people a year in the United States die of rabies, often after being bitten by a wild animal.

Although rabies itself is not the danger it once was, the disease lives on in the public imagination as a terrible threat. A person who is intense about something or very angry is described as "rabid." An enraged person is often described as "foaming at the mouth," in the same way rabies victims produce extra spit, like foam, in their mouths. The word *rabies* comes from a Latin word that means "to rage."

The shadow of a disease like rabies also looms over zombie stories, where a single bite can turn a once-loving friend into a monster.

Louis Pasteur (1822–1895)

Louis Pasteur was born in Dole, France. When he was almost nine, a rabid wolf attacked several people in town. Those people all died, and Louis dreamed of finding a cure for the disease. When he grew up, he earned a degree in science. He developed a method of heating milk to kill bacteria that made people sick. The process is called pasteurization, and we still use it today.

Later in life, Louis turned his attention to rabies, trying to find a cure. On July 6, 1885, a nine-year-old French boy named Joseph became the first patient to receive Louis's new vaccine. Joseph had been badly bitten by a rabid dog. Thanks to the vaccine, which Louis created from a rabies-infected rabbit, Joseph didn't get sick. The disease that had terrified humans for thousands of years was finally beaten. Louis Pasteur became a hero all over the world.

CHAPTER 10
Zombies vs. Kids

In 1992, younger readers got their own zombie story. In *Welcome to Dead House*, Amanda Benson and her brother Josh move into a town called Dark Falls with their parents. The town is eerily quiet and full of shadows. The other kids in town seem nice at first, until Amanda and Josh discover they are, in fact, the living dead.

Welcome to Dead House was a huge hit with young readers, and it turned out to be the first book in a series that's still a bestseller today: Goosebumps, by R. L. Stine. The series began with zombies. More stories about the undead for young readers soon followed.

In *Zombie Chasers*, by John Kloepfer, middle schooler Zack Clarke thinks the biggest thing he has to fear is his older sister Zoe and her friends—until a tasty but deadly fast food called a BurgerDog turns people in his town into zombies. *Zombie Chasers* became another hit series as Zack and his friends struggled to free not just their town but the whole world from the BurgerDog zombie menace.

In The Last Kids on Earth series by Max Brallier, thirteen-year-old Jack Sullivan is one of a small group of kids left after a zombie attack. He and his friends battle the undead and other monsters sent by the evil mastermind

Rezzoch to help him take over the world. The Last Kids on Earth was adapted into an animated series in 2019.

Kids weren't the only ones who wanted to imagine themselves running from zombies. The Japanese company Capcom began developing a video game for adults that let people step into the kind of stories they'd seen on film.

Then, in 2009, the game *Plants vs. Zombies* by PopCap Studios challenged younger players to defend their homes against the invading undead army of the villainous Dr. Zomboss. Their main weapons of defense? Plants with special anti-zombie powers.

Plants vs. Zombies also became a popular comic series in 2013. Readers could follow the adventures of Nate and Patrice, two friends trying to protect their hometown of Neighborville from Dr. Zomboss's hordes.

All these new zombies didn't always follow the rules zombies had in the past. In 2002, the hit movie *28 Days Later* introduced a new kind of monster—the fast zombie who could run and jump. Even today, some zombie fans refuse to consider these creatures zombies. If it didn't shuffle, they believed, it wasn't a zombie!

Zombies running in *28 Days Later*

But most people quickly got used to zombies doing the unexpected. In the 2005 animated movie *Corpse Bride*, a young man accidentally gets engaged to a long-dead girl who has risen from the grave. A few years later, in 2012, the director of *Corpse Bride*, Tim Burton, made *Frankenweenie*.

In that movie, middle schooler Victor Frankenstein is heartbroken when his dog, Sparky, is hit by a car. Inspired by experiments in his science class, he brings Sparky back to life with a jolt of electricity.

Tim Burton (1958–)

Tim Burton grew up in Burbank, California. He loved drawing, painting, and movies. And by the time he was in middle school, he was already making movies in his backyard. Sometimes those movies used stop-motion animation. That meant Tim photographed objects one picture at a time, moving them a tiny bit in between each shot. When the pictures were shown rapidly in order, the objects appeared to be moving. After high school he studied at the California Institute of the Arts and went to work for Walt Disney Productions. He created a short film, *Frankenweenie*, that was an early version of the later 2012 film. It led to him getting to direct his first full-length movie, *Pee-Wee's Big Adventure*. Tim became known for movies that were both spooky and fun, including *Batman*, *The Nightmare Before Christmas*, and *Beetlejuice*.

That same year, *ParaNorman* pitted eleven-year-old Norman Babcock against an army of zombies called from their coffins by a witch.

But zombies and humans weren't always enemies. The 2013 movie *Warm Bodies* tells the story of a zombie whose heart begins to beat again when he falls in love with a human girl. In 2018, the Disney Channel premiered *Zombies*, a musical about a zombie football player who falls for a living cheerleader.

Nicholas Hoult in *Warm Bodies*

Zombies seemed to be everywhere. That made a lot of people wonder: What would they do if zombies actually attacked?

CHAPTER 11
Be Prepared

As fun as it was to fight zombies in video games, some people thought it might be more fun to be a zombie than to fight one. A zombie walk is an event where people dress up like zombies and get together, often for Halloween. They wear tattered clothes and makeup to make it look like they've been dead for a while. The first official zombie walk took place in Toronto in October 2003. It was organized by a local horror movie fan and included only seven people. The idea really caught on, and the walks became a fun way for people to meet other zombie fans. The biggest zombie walk on record was held in 2012 in Buenos Aires, Argentina. It had twenty-five thousand participants.

Zombie Walk in Buenos Aires, Argentina, 2012

Anyone can plan for a zombie attack. In fact, many people have come up with tips for what a person might need to survive in a world full of zombies. These include:

A safe place to live: A strong chain-link fence around a house can keep zombies away. If you live in an apartment, it's better to be on an upper floor.

You can barricade the stairs to keep the zombies from coming up, and turn off the elevator in case one of them hits the right button for your floor by accident.

Food: Stock up on canned food and get a portable stove. Plant a vegetable garden to grow your own food behind your zombie-proof fence.

Water: Use purification tablets and water filters to make water you can drink without getting sick. Use a barrel to collect rainwater.

Electricity: You may need a generator to make electricity. Get one that runs on gasoline for emergencies, but rely on one you can power by pedaling a bicycle.

Medicine: Keep several first aid kits for non-zombie-bite sickness and injuries.

Tools: You'll need a regular toolkit to keep your shelter in good shape, as well as wood and bricks to make repairs. Flashlights are important, as are solar-powered lamps and radios, batteries, and fire extinguishers. A telescope is useful for spotting zombies in the distance. Make sure you keep manuals for how to use and repair everything you have!

Exercise: Keep yourself in shape with regular exercise in case you have to run, and make sure you have some good books and games to play when you're not fighting the undead. But be sure to stay quiet and out of sight. Zombies are attracted to the sight and sound of the living.

Zombie survival kit

Types of Zombies

Zombie stories offer different explanations for how zombies are created, and how you can protect yourself against them.

SUPERNATURAL: The oldest zombie stories are about monsters created through supernatural power. That sometimes means there is a magical way to unmake the zombie as well. According to zombie lore, if a zombie is given salt to eat, he or she will return to the grave.

Example: *I Walked with a Zombie.*

CHEMICAL: Some zombies are created through exposure to strange chemicals that are eaten, breathed in, or touch the skin. These zombies can sometimes be returned to their normal state through a chemical antidote.

Example: *The Zombie Chasers.*

BIOLOGICAL: Biological zombies are infected with an illness. They are very contagious and usually bite. If a cure for the illness is discovered by doctors, they can be stopped.

Example: *Kabaneri of the Iron Fortress.*

EXTRATERRESTRIAL: In some zombie stories, the dead are reanimated by aliens from outer space or other dimensions. To stop the zombies, defeat the aliens.

Example: *The Last Kids on Earth.*

The undead probably don't have much chance
of taking over the world, but they have already
conquered pop culture. Today, zombies are the
stars of horror movies, comedies, action movies,
and even love stories. They're in video games,
books, and comics, and on TV. Their stories are
told almost everywhere around the world.

The mysterious creature that was once known only in the Caribbean and the United States has become one of the world's most well-known nightmares. Shuffling or groaning, shopping or dancing, the zombies are coming. They're hungry—and they can't be stopped.

Timeline of Zombies

1804 — Haiti becomes an independent country, the Republic of Haiti

1885 — A French boy becomes the first person whose life is saved by the rabies vaccine

1929 — The book *The Magic Island* by William Seabrook is published

1932 — The movie *White Zombie* premieres

1940 — Director George A. Romero is born in Bronx, New York

1943 — The movie *I Walked with a Zombie* premieres

1950 — EC begins publishing *Tales from the Crypt*, *The Vault of Horror*, and *The Haunt of Fear*

1968 — *Night of the Living Dead* premieres in Pittsburgh, Pennsylvania

1983 — Michael Jackson's "Thriller" video premieres on MTV

1992 — *Goosebumps #1: Welcome to Dead House* is published

2009 — The videogame *Plants vs. Zombies* is released

2012 — The animated movie *ParaNorman* premieres

2013 — The first issue of the *Plants vs. Zombies* comic book is published

2018 — *Zombies*, a musical TV movie, premieres on the Disney Channel

2024 — EC horror comics relaunch is announced by Oni Press

Timeline of the World

1887 — Construction of the Eiffel Tower begins in Paris, France

1914 — World War I begins in the city of Sarajevo with the assassination of Archduke Franz Ferdinand, heir to the Austro-Hungarian throne

1933 — The first drive-in movie theater opens in Pennsauken Township in Camden, New Jersey. Admission is twenty-five cents per car and per person

1947 — *The Diary of Anne Frank*, the journal of a teenage girl in Amsterdam who died in World War II, is published

1963 — More than 200,000 people gather in Washington, DC, to demand equal rights in the March on Washington

1981 — MTV begins broadcasting music videos twenty-four hours a day

1998 — The Galileo space probe provides evidence that Europa, one of the planet Jupiter's moons, has a liquid ocean under a thick crust of ice

2004 — The social media site Facebook is launched

2019 — The highly contagious coronavirus disease, COVID-19, causes a worldwide pandemic

2024 — A total solar eclipse visible in areas of North America from Mexico to Canada occurs, in which the moon passes in front of the sun for a total of four minutes and twenty-seven seconds

Bibliography

*Books for young readers

*Benson, John, and Bill Mason, editors. ***Vault of Horror, Haunt of Fear, Tales from the Crypt***. West Plains, MO: The Russ Cochran Company, Ltd., 1982.

Bishop, Kyle William. ***American Zombie Gothic: The Rise and Fall (and Rise) of the Walking Dead in Popular Culture***. Jefferson, NC: McFarland & Co., 2010.

*Brallier, Max. ***The Last Kids on Earth and the Zombie Parade***. New York: Viking, 2016.

Brooks, Max. ***The Zombie Survival Guide: Complete Protection from the Living Dead***. New York: Three Rivers Press, 2003.

Futurism. "Body Invaders: Real Zombies in the Animal Kingdom." ***Futurism*** (September 11, 2014).

Gandhi, Lakshmi. "Zoinks! Tracing the History of 'Zombie' from Haiti to the CDC." ***NPR.org*** (December 15, 2013).

George, Nelson, dir. ***Thriller 40***. Sony Music Entertainment, 2023.

Hannan, Brian. "Behind the Scenes: *Night of the Living Dead* (1968)." ***The Magnificent 60s Blog*** (September 26, 2022).

*Kloepfer, John. *The Zombie Chasers*. New York: HarperCollins, 2010.

Louissaint, Guilberly. "What Is Haitian Voodoo?" *The Conversation* (August 21, 2019).

Luckhurst, Roger. *Zombies: A Cultural History*. London: Reaktion Books, 2015.

Muncer, Mike. *The Evolution of Horror Podcast*. Season 4, episode 123.

Nugent, Connie, Gilbert Berdine, and Kenneth Nugent. "The Undead in Culture and Science." *Baylor University Medical Center Proceedings* 38 (2) (April 2018).

Pegg, Simon. "The Dead and the Quick." *The Guardian* (November 3, 2008).

*Stine, R. L. *Goosebumps: Welcome to Dead House*. New York: Scholastic, 1992.

Waskik, Bill, and Monica Murphy. *Rabid: A Cultural History of the World's Most Diabolical Virus*. New York: Penguin Publishing Group, 2012.

WHOHQ

YOUR HEADQUARTERS FOR HISTORY

Activities, Mad Libs, and sidesplitting jokes!
Discover the Who HQ books beyond the biographies

Who? What? Where?

Learn more at whohq.com!